My Trunk

By Cameron Macintosh

I have a big trunk!

My trunk is long and thick.

trunk

My trunk is very strong.

It can pick up lots of things.

It can pick up big things
like planks and logs.

log

I can sniff and smell things with my trunk.

Sniff! Sniff!

I can call with it, too!

Honk!

I can drink from the bank.

I dunk my trunk!

With my trunk, I can get things to snack on.

It can yank bits off!

Yum!

I can swing my trunk
to get rid of bugs!

Bonk!

I can link my trunk
with my pal.

I love my big, strong trunk!

CHECKING FOR MEANING

1. What does the elephant's trunk look like? *(Literal)*

2. What are three things an elephant can do with its trunk? *(Literal)*

3. Do you think a trunk is helpful for an elephant? Why? *(Inferential)*

EXTENDING VOCABULARY

planks	What are *planks*? What is another word that has a similar meaning?
bank	What is the meaning of the word *bank* in this text? Is there another meaning of this word? Can you use the word in a sentence to show this other meaning? E.g. We put my money in the *bank*.
dunk	What does *dunk* mean? What word could replace *dunk* in this text? E.g. dip, splash.

MOVING BEYOND THE TEXT

1. Where can you see elephants? Have you been to a zoo or a wildlife park where they live?

2. Talk about what elephants eat. How do they find food?

3. What do we call a group of elephants? Do they live in these groups?

4. How are people helping to care for elephants in the wild?

SPEED SOUNDS

ft	mp	nd	nk	st

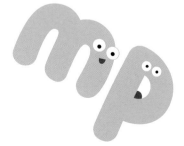

PRACTICE WORDS

planks

trunk

Honk

drink

bank

dunk

yank

Bonk

and

link